SUE QUINONES

ANGELBABY

A True Story Of Faith, Miracles, And The Supernatural

Arika With Sunflowers   *Chalk Drawing*   **Jose Luis Quinones**

Sue Quinones

Copyright © 2021 Sue Quinones, Susan Quinones
All Rights Reserved

I would like to happily acknowledge my years of recording my daughter Arika's life and publishing her interesting journey with her gracious help.

All rights reserved, including the right to reproduce this book, paintings, prints, or drawings, or portion thereof or any form whatsoever including audio rights without the written consent of author Sue Quinones, Susan Quinones

Exterior and Interior Design Sue Quinones
Drawings Sue Quinones and Jose Luis Quinones
suequinones.com and joseluisquinones.com

Exterior Cover / Back Cover Jose Luis Quinones
Technical and Digital Expertise John Bucce

ISBN 9798537059776 First Edition Paperback

Published in the United States of America
Sue Quinones P.O. Box 31214, Independence, Ohio 44131

ANGELBABY

Thanks to God for placing an authentic life-changing experience in our path. We are blessed

***

I want to dedicate this book to my loving husband, Jose. My exceptional children Andrea, Alena, Andrew, and Arika and adorable grandchildren giving me a reason to live. I love them all forever and a day.

***

Thanks to my family of editors. A special thanks to my brother John for all his digital and technical support, as always. His kind heart is what life is all about!

***

A special thanks to the biological parents who unknowingly gave birth to an extraordinary child.

Table of Contents

Chapter 1	Before Angels	1
Chapter 2	Angel On Our Doorstep	7
Chapter 3	Revelation	13
Chapter 4	The Early Years	23
Chapter 5	Seeing Spirits	41
Chapter 6	Arika Goes to School	53
Chapter 7	Fish Tales	63
Chapter 8	Rosa The Pig	73
Chapter 9	Angels Outside The Doors	81
Chapter 10	Others With Gifts	87
Chapter 11	Miracle On Delta Flight 1230	101
Chapter 12	The Gifts Flourish	109

Introduction

Parenting is the most significant thankless job in the world, but it can be rewarding. You are caring for a precious child and protecting them from harm. Your job is to keep them alive for their entire lives. You are also guiding your child to strive to help them to become a meaningful part of society.

We thought we were up for the challenge. Our family was fortunate enough to adopt two exceptional children: the first, a three-year-old boy, and the second and last child, a baby girl.

We were ready to care for children with learning disabilities, delays, or issues. It was a reality of the job of parenting. Instead, the baby girl surprised us with an experience of a lifetime, including supernatural gifts from God.

This book is a journey into the enigmatic territory of the true meaning of faith, miracles, and the unknown. Does God choose specific people to help us take a glimpse into the mysteries of life, allowing us to heal our faith? Is it all coincidence or not? Please judge for yourself.

SUE QUINONES

Chapter 1

Before Angels

Brilliant red geraniums lined the cast iron railing on the porch of our enormous old house. I silently sat, watching the hummingbirds sip on the sugar water concoction my husband Jose had mixed for them. The hummingbird's wings moved so swiftly. They were on the verge of being invisible to my eyes. At that moment, I wondered perhaps if hummingbird wings might be comparable to angel wings. I guess I would never know or, so I thought.

As a young child growing up in Cleveland, Ohio, I found myself, my sisters, and brothers raised by our parents in a happy, healthy environment. We were middle-class Catholics. Our Mother stayed home as a caregiver, as was the norm during the mid-twentieth century. Dad worked as the breadwinner. Our family was a stable and loving unit of seven.

My Mother had a disease similar to muscular dystrophy. It never seemed to hinder her ability to care for all five of us children. She had several corrective surgeries requiring hospital stays throughout our childhood. We went to different relative's homes during her operations. As I became a teen, I would take charge of the children for my Mom. I had a motherly personality and would handle unexpected tasks with my siblings without even thinking about it.

My Dad was a wonderful father. He had a kind heart but a stern presence. He never had to spank us. We were not terrible children at all, but we feared my Dad. If we did something wrong, Mom would say, "Wait until your father comes home." Expecting Dad to come home was punishment enough.

After work, Dad's car would pull in the elongated driveway, lengthening our thoughts of discipline. His big steel-toed work boots had iron filings covering them from the foundry. He was close when you heard his boots pound on the cement. Dad would clean them, so he would not drag the mess into the house. He would then sit on the stairs and remove his boots. Most of the time, Dad never said a word after being tired from the long day with all his supervisor responsibilities. I walked with him to the house in silence. However, we did scatter like insects, far away from the wrath of what we thought he might do if any of us were in trouble.

Dad was an excellent provider, father, and husband. He loved my Mom. Every Sunday, Dad took us children to church, even if Mom could not come. We all sat in the pews, counting the small patterned crosses by the back wall behind the altar. We argued over who counted them correctly. All of us couldn't wait to come home for Mom's freshly prepared crepes filled with jam and whipped cream. What a reward for sitting so long in church!

We always had plenty to eat, but you wouldn't think so by how all of us children appeared. As a preteen, I was tall and skinny for my age, as were my sisters and brothers. I was one of the five-string bean children. We all got along well and seldom disagreed.

Everyone loved Mom and Dad. Mom was beautiful, innocent, naive, and happy. Mom spent most of her time in a wheelchair, cooking, cleaning, and caring for us as we all grew up. She loved children and would have a million if she could. As I became a teen, I often marveled at how two people could love each other so much. I hoped someday I would get married and have a terrific family like ours.

Sometimes Mom would relax by sketching pictures of the Blessed Virgin Mother. I loved to watch her draw. Talented in the arts also, I pursued a career as an artist and eventually became an art instructor. As a young adult, I would spend hours drawing after school and into the evening in my attic bedroom. Being left alone to do artwork gave me much time to think about everything in the world.

Death was what I feared most—also wondering what happened after you die. I would think about religion and its purpose like it was a fried bologna sandwich so easy to digest. Guess it was much more complicated than I initially thought. As a young teen, I figured if you dressed up, went to church, and tried not to fall asleep, you would go to heaven!

I drifted away from believing in religion altogether when I graduated from Cooper School of Art, Cleveland Institute of Art, and Case Western Reserve University. Maybe it was a combination of college classes questioning the reality of faith itself.

I thought God was a crutch for humanity. What about all the cruel things he did to people? How could I still believe? A bit of me always deemed religion authentic since most of the world still had unconditional faith. Could they all be wrong?

My boyfriend, Jose, now my husband, believed in God. Yet, I never discussed my skepticism of religion. Jose and I were both from large families and decided to have many children. We agreed we would raise our children according to the Catholic faith.

Our first child was Andrea, then came Alena. They were our pride and joy! I had trouble with my pregnancies, and we adopted the rest of the children. Andrew was three when we embraced him into the family. He was vivacious, adorable, and spirited. Andrew needed the most attention. We put off having more children for some time and thought we would stop. Little did we know we all would be in for a big surprise.

SUE QUINONES

Chapter 2

Angel On Our Doorstep

It was early summer, and our family spent the day together. We went to the West Side Market on West 25th Street in Cleveland. There was a festival. Outside of the building were many vendors. One woman was sitting there with a tiny handmade sign, *Psychic Readings,* five dollars.

We had no interest, but my husband thought it would be fun. We were hungry and went into the building to eat. After the reading, Jose came in to see the rest of the festivities. People in the market were like ants on an anthill scurrying around searching for food at different locations. With arms full of various cheeses and fruits, we had our fill of the day's offerings.

On our way outside, we all saw the psychic woman still sitting there. I asked my husband, "Did she say anything important?" Jose smiled and replied, "She told me we would have a baby in September." My family burst out laughing at the thought. They all knew I had a hysterectomy at thirty-seven and could not have any more children. Laughing, I stated, "Well, I think you wasted your five dollars!"

It was early September when the telephone rang. I got a phone call from Catholic Charities. Why did they call us? How did they know? Lorain County asked us if we wanted to adopt a Hispanic baby girl. We had intended to accept an older child around five to eight years old. The adoption application and home study were complete. We had not started searching for a child yet.

I couldn't believe this miracle was all happening. People wait years on a list for a baby! How did we become so privileged? The social worker said the mother read our profile and thought we would be the correct placement for her baby. The biological mother had many problems to deal with in her life. What a selfless act for a woman to give up her child for adoption so this baby might have a better life experience. To this day, I am forever grateful for her sacrifice.

Time had passed since adopting Andrew. He was now fourteen, Andrea was already eighteen, and Alena was sixteen years old. Jose and I were now in our mid-forties and had decided it was getting a little late in life for any young infant, but we were still open to the idea. We sat down and had a family meeting to see if we should even consider it. We wrote the pros and cons of adding a young new member. Andrea was the most against adding more children, but her heart almost melted when she got to hold the baby for the first time.

We went to the foster home visitation and met the baby girl. She was a beautiful Hispanic-looking child. My teacher's instinct took over to analyze her every movement, checking every ounce of her body. I clicked my fingers together, studying to see if her eyes followed the sound to test her hearing. I noticed her hands were not closed like babies naturally are. Her palms were extended as if she was praying to God. I thought maybe she had a slight motor delay or a health condition unknown to me.

Looking up, I took a deep breath and said, "Oh well, God. Here we go again!" I felt I would take on anything that God would throw our way, hoping he would help us if something were wrong with her. Fortunately, she had no delays or significant issues. We couldn't help but fall in love with her. She had thick hair. It looked like she was wearing a big black curly mop on her head. She did not look like she was two months old. Her eyes were pools of dark brown, and her skin was a beautiful tan that gave her a healthy glow.

Her name was Erica. We loved the name. It was a firm name and seemed to fit her well. All our children's names started with the letter "A," so we renamed her Arika upon finalizing the adoption. We did not want Arika to feel out of place in the family. The pronunciation was still the same.

My oldest daughter Andrea took her turn to hold Arika. She wasn't sure we should adopt another child after Andrew. He was quite a handful to raise. The baby looked up at Andrea and started cooing at her butterfly necklace. It looked like Arika was carrying a conversation with the beautiful insect about the whole adoption thing. We all laughed, and then I said, "Wow, I think that is a sign that she will love to talk." I was right!

Since all of our children had the same initials, we assigned a symbol to fit their personality or demeanor. We used these icons to denote possession, for example, labeling toothbrushes or book bags. Andrea had a heart logo because she was kindhearted. Alena had the symbol of a star being a superstar in cheerleading and track. Andrew had a lightning bolt because he was a daredevil. I don't know which one of us said it, but since Arika had talked with the butterfly necklace, we decided right there at the foster home to give her a butterfly symbol.

Arika bonded with all of us, acting as if she was always part of our family. None of us wanted to depart from the foster home without her. Proud Jose was already taking photographs while everyone took turns holding their new sibling.

Then it was my turn. Alena brought a paper pad taking notes while I asked the foster mom about Arika's habits, feeding schedule, and naptime. The foster mom told me to bring a set of clothes for Arika. The dress she was wearing was part of her collection for the children she had watched throughout the years.

It was time to leave the foster home and our baby until we came back to pick her up for good. It was hard not to run out the door with Arika. We already thought she was ours. We had to leave her one last time.

After leaving the foster parents heading home, all we could think about was Arika. We had given away all the baby things from years ago and needed to start over again. Our family went straight to the store with a list of clothes and items we might need. Jose and I took our *grown babies* shopping for our *new baby* girl. Our family felt blessed by God, everything was falling into place, but nothing we did would prepare us for what was to come. We had no clue how special Arika truly was.

Chapter 3

Revelation

My Mother lived with us and cared for Arika while my husband and I went to work. Arika was now two years old. She was tired from playing with her dog, Rosie. Mom laid her on the couch in the sunroom for a nap. She would sit in the room guarding watch over Arika while having a cup of coffee.

Arika had been sleeping for about an hour. Suddenly, a white glowing light appeared above Arika. Startled, Mom tried to awaken her. Arika opened her eyes and glanced up at the white light, and said, "Look at the beautiful angels." The bright glow emanated for a few minutes then disappeared. My Mother couldn't wait for me to get home. I was skeptical. How could Arika say that? She didn't even know what an angel was! She was only two. Is my Mother becoming senile?

Being doubtful, I started analyzing the situation and watching my Mom and Arika. My Mother seemed fine, but now, Arika talked to someone or something throughout the day. Did she have an imaginary friend? Could she have schizophrenia? There were no signs of this behavior before.

I analyzed her every move, questioning Arika as not to suggest what she was seeing. With caution, I asked her, "Who are you talking to, baby?" Arika replied, "Angels, Mommy." Asking Arika the same thing every day, she would respond with the same answer. Some days it was one or two angels. On other days Arika would see more angels, many more.

I had been taking notes on everything Arika had said for quite some time. Weeks had now passed since the first angel observation, and she was still seeing angels. I did not see her talk to angels on Sundays and thought maybe she did, and I didn't notice.

So, one Sunday, I confronted Arika, asking if she saw any angels. She said no. Then Arika revealed, "They are in heaven being humble to God." Humble! Where did she get that word? We never say that. She was only two! When you asked Arika about the angels, her reaction was always the same. She alleged, "God gave me special eyes." How does she even know who God is? The hair stood up on my arms, and chills went down my spine from her sincere statements.

Since Arika's arrival into our family, strange little things started transpiring that I could not explain, but I couldn't deny they happened. The first thing was the numbers 111, 222, 333, 444, 555, 1111, showing up in our house and even at work. If I looked up at the clock, it was triple or even quadruple numbers. It was not as if I stared at the clock all day. If I used the microwave, I would turn to see if my food was heated enough. I would see

1:11 left on the timer. I would watch a movie and stop it to retrieve a snack. It was precisely 4:44 on the video indicator near the bottom of the screen.

At school, a student needed a hall pass to the media center. I looked up at the digital clock on my desk. It was 11:11. Later that day, a second student asked for a pass to the office, and the time was 2:22. What is going on? It was happening every day. How could this just be a coincidence? It seemed unlikely.

My sister Joanne and her husband Tom visited for the day. She noticed the repeated numbers. I did not tell her about what I was seeing. My husband and children saw them too. To this day, we still experience the number phenomenon all day long, every day.

When you research numerology, numbers represent new beginnings, protection, a wake-up call from the universe, or being surrounded by angels and guides. If you see numbers repeating on the same day, it means a spiritual awakening. When Arika was older, she told Jose and me that God surrounds and protects our house all the time.

The second strange incident occurred when I was tucking Arika in her upstairs bedroom at night. I was reading her a book and saying prayers. She said, "Mommy, I can see the VCR downstairs, and it is 8-3-5." Could she see things remotely from one area to another? That would be crazy! There were not any clocks in her bedroom. I dashed into my bedroom to see the time, and it was 8:35. On many occasions, Arika could see visions from far away. It was incredible. How could Arika do that? It sure seemed like she saw things from a distance.

Remote viewing is the paranormal ability to see across distances without physically traveling there. With this ability, one can see across time and space without being present. According to online sources, it takes years to train a person to learn remote viewing and improve accuracy. Well, Arika did it in about one second, and did I mention she is a toddler? Once these brief events started, I thought I better write them down.

Arika's experience shocked me at that moment. I pondered how a baby could see across to another location? Could this Extra Sensory Perception *(E.S.P.)* belief be valid? My skepticism was preventing me from believing what my eyes had seen. After the first time, I still documented and witnessed multiple in-person accounts of Arika's many unusual perceptions. I realize you were not there to witness this unique phenomenon, but it was not a coincidence! She had the gift of angels and remote viewing.

Jose walked into the room on another occasion while Arika played with a rosary and a snow globe. As Arika was studying it, Jose asked Arika for fun, "What was Uncle Victor doing right now?" Arika replied, "He is making a sandwich." Jose took his cell phone and called his brother in Texas. Jose inquired, "What are you doing right now?" Victor had just finished making a sandwich and was ready to eat it. Jose told Victor what Arika had said. They were both shocked. Victor is halfway across the United States. I would say that it was a remote viewing or the greatest guess ever!

Our son, Andrew, was in the Marines, and I hadn't heard from him in over four months. I was fearful they had shipped him to Iraq, Iran, or Afghanistan. I said nothing in front of Arika as not to alarm her.

We went to Florida to visit relatives, and while eating dinner at Applebee's restaurant, my sister-in-law Gladys asked about Andrew. Arika told everyone at the round table to hold hands. She then bowed her head and disclosed, "Dear God, please tell Andrew to call mom. She needs to talk to him." Everyone at the table looked surprised. Madeline lowered her head quickly. My niece Jenny curiously made eye contact with Arika looking perplexed that a young kid would ask them to hold hands and pray for Andrew to call.

Two hours later, on that same day, Andrew called. I felt relieved to hear his voice. He said, "Hi, Mom! I don't know why I called right now. It just kind of popped into my head!

I had spent the last several years recording Arika's exciting moments, visions, events, and feelings, including when Arika saved us from having a car accident. One of the most memorable times was with her sister Alena.

When Arika was three, she told Alena that she would die if she sat on a horse. I freaked out with this little child saying something so terrifying. I remember exclaiming, "Baby, don't say that!" Arika answered, "Okay, mommy."

We tried to forget about it, but I never let Alena go horseback riding. I remember paranoia setting in and telling Alena not to even sit on a merry-go-round. I did not understand what Arika's message meant.

A few years went by, and Alena hurried away to college. She kept getting sick and went to the hospital several times. I knew that the *sitting on a horse; you will die* scenario was as fresh in my mind as it was the first time Arika had said it. Could a three-year-old be correct? I investigated the possibility of a connection between her illness and Arika's ominous prediction of doom.

I took Alena to an allergist and had her tested with a complete allergy profile. Without knowing the prophecy Arika had said, I hoped the doctor would put this nonsense to rest. The doctor's face looked surprised. Alena had a huge welt on her back where the test area was. He had seen no one so allergic to horses! I told the doctor Alena's college was out in the country. Farms surrounded her with many horses and cows in the neighboring fields. Could that get her so sick? He felt the allergy test warranted a complete avoidance of horses from now on. Contact could be deadly.

I thought back to when Alena was a baby. She would always have trouble breathing. Alena gasped for air while I nursed her on our beautiful sofa. Every night she would cry herself to sleep while struggling to breathe.

It was an antique sofa, and yes, it was old, and when I had it reupholstered years later, the man told me it was an original Victorian couch. The stuffing was horsehair. Back in the day, that is what furniture makers used to place inside the cushions. She was sick throughout her childhood and had breathing issues. Without knowing, I tortured my baby Alena because she was allergic to the horsehair in my couch.

After that incident, anytime Arika would talk, we listened. Her nickname became known as AngelBaby. We guarded her with our lives. To protect Arika, I made up a saying to surround her with angels when she went to sleep. We still use this all-encompassing phrase to this day at bedtime. We also apply various versions of this saying when traveling because it makes you feel so safe.

God, please surround Arika with angels to protect her in the day and night. Amen.

Arika was always solemn in demeanor, but one time she caught me off guard. Arika said, "Mom, do you know that boy angels can take off their heads?" With a puzzled look, I said. "They can?" She giggled, replying, "Yes, the boys take their heads off to impress the girl angels." We laughed as I shook my head at the silliness of the whole idea.

Chapter 4

The Early Years

It took a village to watch over our AngelBaby. Between all of us, we had to share taking care of Arika. We didn't know how to raise a *Heavenly Gifted Child*. There was not a book anywhere that told us how to keep her safe from the unknown. We saw no spirits, ghosts, or any otherworldly presence until Arika joined our lives.

We had the baby monitor on at all times when she was in the crib. Having a toddler with such a gift was terrifying, overwhelming, but amazing. With all the good came some bad or unusual. Arika was like a conduit where spirits came to visit her and bridge the gap between the two dimensions.

Arika seemed to attract many entities. She was not fearful of life forces if they had positive energy. One evening Arika could not sleep. She cried because she saw a dark, cynical soul. She slept with us until Andrea came home. The following week she slept with Alena. It was the first time it shocked her. The entity must have been ominous. I lay sleepless, worrying about what Arika must have seen. When Arika was older, she learned to put her hand up in the air, instructing the dark images never to return.

One day I was walking upstairs on the second floor of our home. In the hallway, I saw a large gray mist come from the laundry room. It slithered right in front of me and up into the hall light fixture socket. The apparition disappeared. I was reluctant to tell anyone for fear that they might ridicule me.

Two weeks later, Andrea told me she saw a large gray mist upstairs at the end of the same hallway go right into the light fixture. We discussed negative energy ramifications, trying to approach, influence, or attach itself to Arika. Andrea and I decided we needed Holy Water to bless the entire house from top to bottom. We didn't know what else to do.

In 1858 in Lourdes, France, *The Blessed Virgin Mary* appeared to a fourteen-year-old girl gathering firewood with her sister and friend. Her name was Bernadette Soubirous. She witnessed the Marian apparitions. Later in life, Bernadette was canonized as a Catholic saint.

We all went as a family to the Roman Catholic Lady of Lourdes religious shrine in Euclid, Ohio. There is an area with a small stone gifted from France at the Ohio shrine. It is embedded in a tiny embossed cross. To the right is spring water streaming over the other little pebble that the *Blessed Virgin Mary* once stood. Now the blessed water flows upon the small rock where you can collect the Holy Water in a bottle to take with you. Others put the sacred water on themselves in hopes of a miracle. Our Euclid shrine is fortunate enough to possess some crucial pieces of stone from France.

Many miracles occurred at the shrine. There is a glass-enclosed display case with documentation of these marvels. People come to the shrine to surround themselves with the entire religious experience. They drink the blessed Holy Water in the hope of a miracle.

We went to the shrine for the first time with Arika. As we approached the memorial, she was visibly smiling. AngelBaby could not wait to tell us that there were hundreds of angels there. This place was such a comfort to Arika that we would often go to the shrine in place of going to church. Arika felt at peace and seemed at home with all of her angels. There was an area to place blessed candles. Arika would tell us where to put them. She would squeal with excitement, "Right here! That's where an angel is."

We brought a few large plastic bottles and filled them with the Holy Water. When we got home, Andrea, Jose, and I put the blessed water into spray bottles and started in the attic, working our way into the basement. We prayed to *The Hail Mary* and *Our Father* as we progressed, spraying every inch of the house.

Since blessing the house, we did not see any evil apparitions. Arika would view a man outside the home, walking up and down the driveway. After applying the Holy Water, we saw nothing ominous in the house as long as we lived there.

Before we blessed the house, toddler Arika recalled a scary entity. AngelBaby described evil eyes in our wood-burning fireplace as she sat in her playpen. It must have left quite an impression for her to remember this incident when she was so young.

When older, Arika would recall the event and the terrifying moment that was etched in her memory. As an afterthought writing this, I never blessed the fireplace inside with Holy Water opening into the chimney. It allowed a malicious spirit to enter—what a sneaky creature.

It was time for AngelBaby to move from the crib to the bed. As Arika turned three, she started describing another strange phenomenon. Arika saw white flowing images every night describing the shapes with her hands. They were white blobs moving back and forth everywhere. Arika couldn't sleep because the forms captivated her thoughts.

Andrea and Alena took turns sleeping with her for a while. We left the lights on, so Arika would not focus on the white forms moving all night. She was never afraid of them, just annoyed. Arika came to grips with the mysterious configurations. Over time, the silhouettes slowed down, and she could see them better.

Arika exclaimed, "Angels and spirits! That's what they are!" I retorted, "How do you know the difference between them, Arika? Is there a difference between angels and spirits?" Arika alleged, "Angels never touch the ground. They hover. You never see their feet." Arika took a deep breath and seemed disgusted that I did not know the difference. She reiterated, "Angel's hover. Spirits stand right in front of you and can see them to their toes."

One night we tucked Arika in bed. She was talking to someone. Andrea overheard her on the baby monitor. It was Andrea's turn to check on her. As she entered the room, Andrea questioned Arika, "Who are you talking to, AngelBaby?" Arika pointed to the closet, so Andrea opened the door. Arika verbalized, "It's my friend Eddie! He is dead." Andrea said she shivered with fear at the thought she would see a spirit in the closet. Andrea was thankful she saw nothing.

At a young age, Arika would look at my *H. W. Janson's, History Of Art* book from my classes at Cooper School of Art. She would view the drawings on various pages. Arika would study the chapter on architecture in the old Gothic Cathedrals with their vaulted ceilings and ornate interiors. I thought it was strange that this little child would concentrate on these boring black and white photos. You would assume she would look at the colorful artwork.

What was Arika thinking? Did she see something that I could not see? Later on, when Arika was a teenager, these church interiors would symbolize her search for a church that made her feel comfortable to attend. We would visit various locations. Some churches Arika said didn't have angels in them. We traveled from one church and then another in search of a good fit for our family.

One day, we visited St. Stanislaus Church in Slavic Village, Cleveland, Ohio. Arika said this church had many angels in it. She also noted that angels were guarding some statues. I thought this was strange. Why would an angel protect these figurines? It just did not seem it was the norm?

Through the church brochure, I found out that some figurines had reliquary boxes containing relics of saints. Relics could be bones, objects associated with the saint, or clothing pieces. They tucked others in niches around the main altar and additional locations in the church.

The church's relics were associated with *The True Cross of Christ, Saint Stanislaus* (1969), *Saint John Vianney, Saint Pius X, Saint Bonaventure, Saint Francis, Saint Anthony, and St. Gemma Galgani.* The altar of sacrifice contained relics of *Saint Innocent* and *Saint Donatus. Cardinal Stanislaus Dziwisz* presented a relic of Saint John Paul II in 2014 during a pastoral visit to St. Stanislaus Church.

The most celebrated was *Cardinal Karol, Wojtyla,* then *Pope John Paul II,* in 1969. His Holiness gifted a relic of *St. Stanislaus* to the Polish community of Cleveland. I guess all those relics of saints were sacred enough to warrant guarding by countless angels of God.

Arika also told me St. Stanislaus Church made her feel calm when entering through the big wooden doors. Sometimes she could feel a vibration as she approached the interior where the angels would greet her. I guess my *H. W. Janson's History Of Art* volume came in handy to help Arika find the church from her childhood picture book!

It seemed like Arika was always thinking and never at a loss for words. She would talk about the strangest things when she was playing. Arika told me several times, when she was two years old until four or five, how much she missed her ancestors in Puerto Rico. At first, I didn't comprehend what she was saying. How could this little girl look sad, sigh with a sadness in her voice, and say, "I miss my ancestors in Puerto Rico! I miss all of my other ancestors everywhere!" How did she even know what an ancestor was? I listened to her every word and wrote it down.

Later on, I read an article about young children telling their parents information about their lives before being born and in heaven. It made me think about Arika remembering her encounters in heaven, which I could not prove, but neither could I disprove it to the world.

Arika would inform us of her time in heaven. She would be missing people on the other side. I remember AngelBaby would tell us how God chose her to be our baby. Arika seemed to know some inside information about heaven. One day I asked Arika, "What happens to you when you go to heaven?" She replied, "When they open the gate, you see all your ancestors who died." Arika told me she was not afraid to die because she realized her spirit would always be there. Our bodies are just a softshell and not important — what a strange statement coming from this little child.

When young, Arika revealed her random thoughts again and said, "Mom. Did you know God said it was my destiny to go to another family, but he gave me to you?" The weirdest thing was that I told no one, not even my husband, about the upsetting news of someone else adopting her.

Catholic Charities called and said that there was a young couple available to take Arika instead. They had been waiting for a baby for a long time. I begged the social worker to please reconsider. She was required to show them the background information on Arika first. The telephone rang, and the adoption specialist told us the other couple had changed their mind. She approved us, and Arika became our child. The adoption was divine intervention at its best.

One day my Mom and I were watching Arika and Rosie, our Labrador, playing with bubbles. She had a bubble maker that shot bubbles into the air. Arika laughed so hard as she watched her dog. Rosie would leap up and eat the bubbles. Rosie and Arika took turns consuming them. They ate enough bubbles to float. Arika told me about heaven and how beautiful it was. As she stared at the glistening bubbles, I remember Arika saying, "The colors in heaven are more beautiful than the colors here on earth." Why would she say that? How could she know?

Watching Arika brought so much joy to my mother, who was still lonely because of her husband's loss and now recently her sister Louise. As we sat on the porch, that little four-year-old said to my mom, "This Taco Bell shirt I am wearing today is from Aunt Louise. She gave it to me. I miss her." My Mom spoke with sorrow in her voice, "I miss her too."

Arika placed her little hand on my Mom's hand and stated, "Don't be sad. You had your sister for a lifetime and had lots of fun memories. Now she has to go to heaven with Papa." (My Dad) I couldn't believe a small child could comprehend such an advanced concept. It takes adults a lifetime to understand the notion of death.

Arika also told me, "Mom, you know when you die, you get to do anything you want. Aunt Louise was having a good time in heaven because she was busy cleaning." I laughed because I remembered back when my Aunt was alive; she bought a striking emerald ring. Aunt Louise said she liked to mop the kitchen while wearing that ring because it sparkled and looked shiny when she cleaned!

Arika saw a ring my mother was wearing and asked to put it on. She placed the ring on her finger. Arika informed us it belonged to Weasey. It was a ring my Aunt Louise gave to my Mom. My mother looked shocked. That was my Aunt's nickname when she was young. We never told Arika her nickname or ever mentioned it before. How did Arika know? There were so many things she knew.

Arika, Mom, Andrea, and I went to eat lunch at a restaurant. AngelBaby always sat with Andrea. Arika said she needed to sit with my Mom because Aunt Louise was seated next to her. Arika said she didn't understand why her aunt wouldn't talk. Andrea and I speculated that maybe Aunt Louise was in transition somehow and unable to communicate yet with Arika.

We had a pond in our sunroom that my husband and children gave me for Mother's Day. They bought and named three goldfish after an American children's cartoon called *Powerpuff Girls*. Bubbles, Blossom, and Buttercup occupied the new pond. We also had rocks in the water for decoration. There was one rock my Mom put in the small pool from my Aunt Louise's house. It was like a keepsake from times past.

Arika was fascinated with the fish and the water. She stared into the pond and said, "I hear echoes of Aunt Louise." I inquired, "Arika, what do you mean by echoes?" She replied, "When you throw a rock into the water, it makes circles that get bigger and bigger, and that's where I hear Aunt Louise."

Jose was a great dad for Arika. She waited for Jose to come home for their daily walk across the street to the Metroparks. Arika and Rosie would get ready for their new adventure. Jose always had a smile on his face. He was toting his Nikon camera for the numerous pictures he would take of Arika and Rosie.

As she approached an old oak tree, Arika would untie her invisible horse and jump on and gallop the entire way. Jose stayed in shape, trying to keep up with her adventures while photographing everything. Arika would tie her horse up at the bench where she rested for a little while and picked flowers for me before the trip home. The bond was great between them. She always called him *Big Guy,* even though he was only five feet six inches tall.

Arika saw the spirit of Jose's dad in the park. Jose's father had died over twenty-five years before Arika's birth. She told Jose that his father was standing toward a grouping of bushes. Jose said, "What should I do to see him?" She suggested, "Invite him to come home with us." Jose asked his father to come home, even though he couldn't see him. Once they arrived home, Jose forgot to tell me about his father being invited to our house.

That night Alena and Andrea slept in the sunroom. During the night, they saw a figure of a man in the room. The two girls shivered, covering their heads with the blankets until they drifted off to sleep.

The next day after the girl's terrifying visitor, I asked Arika about her park adventure. She explained, "I saw dad's father. It's the same person in the picture in the sunroom." The only photograph in the house was in that room. Jose's Uncle Bilo gave it to him as a present. It was a photo of Jose's dad. His father had died before Arika was born, and she never met him. At that moment, I realized the spirit that Alena and Andrea saw was Jose's father. Jose invited his father into our home when they were at the park, and his dad was only making his presence known to the girls.

During another walk with Jose, Arika galloped on her invisible horse and paused from her ride. She turned and looked at Jose, smiling, and said, "Dad, do you remember when your van wheels fell off?" Jose responded. "Yes." Then he realized the accident occurred over ten years ago. Arika was not even born when that van mishap occurred. Jose could not wait to tell me. When he got home, he checked his current vehicle. Jose came into the house with a smile on his face. The tie rods on my van were in terrible shape and ready to break. Jose boasted, "Arika saved me from an accident."

Arika never cried, even as a baby. She went to bed every night after her bath with no trouble or complaints. Most of the time, she hurried away to bed, saying, "I'm tired, goodnight."

AngelBaby was just like any other child; she could be mischievous. I had just arrived at my mom's house to pick up Arika after work. She and Rosie disappeared. I walked down the hall and smelled the perfume, *White Diamonds*. I called out

Arika's name, and it was silent. Rosie and Arika peaked their head out by the bed's side, covered with expensive white talc powder from head to toe. Arika found my mother's fancy puff with the overpowering scent from the aromatic dust.

I remember how much Arika loved Rosie. She played with the dog as if it was a sibling. Arika thought that she was a dog. The rest of her sisters and brother were grown-up, and Rose became her buddy. AngelBaby had a great imagination. She named her dog Eric and herself Nik Nik. Every day they would go on another imaginary adventure.

One evening, after Arika finished playing with Rosie, she told me to call Aunt Nilda in Florida. Arika explained that Jose's sister had three angels watching over her. Two outside the door of her house and one in her bedroom. Jose called and told his sister what Arika had said. Nilda laughed, declaring, "A few days ago, I felt something touch my face. I thought it was an angel." Nilda prayed for God to send her an angel to protect her house during the recent hurricane. Arika's message thrilled Nilda because God had sent her three angels.

It was summer, and Arika and I were doing errands all over town. We went down Granger Road hill toward Canal Road in the Valley View, Cuyahoga Valley, Ohio. The majestic I-480 bridge hovers way up in the sky at 212 feet (64.62m) in height. I don't know if you have ever driven across that area before, but it is terrifying. The bridge rails are low, with worthless thin fencing surrounding the edges. People move so fast, and I will admit, I follow suit out of fear, trying to get to the end without dying.

One time I saw a semi-truck dangling off the side of the bridge. I couldn't believe it did not fall. As we faced the bridge on Canal Road, Arika looked up and shouted, "There is a giant angel on the 480-bridge walking back and forth protecting the people driving!" I told Arika that I felt sorry for the giant angel—what a crazy job!

Arika became Andrea's sidekick while Alena was away at college. Alena was finishing her doctorate in Pharmacy at Ohio Northern University. While Andrea read by the fireplace, Arika sat on Andrea's lap to read a book. I was sitting in a chair at the far end of the room, watching the fireplace's embers flicker.

Both girls were both deep in thought, twirling their hair and lost in their reading when Arika demanded, "Andrea, put your hand up in the air!" Andrea followed Arika's directive. Andrea said, "What was that? It felt like a cool mist." Arika responded, "It was a halo of an angel."

Andrea had fallen asleep on the sunroom couch when Arika called her to see more angels. Andrea saw three small lights about the size of a silver dollar. Andrea tried to investigate the incident with skepticism to disprove what her eyes wanted her to believe as a trained science teacher.

Light surrounded the sunroom on the three walls lined with windows. She cupped her hands around the white glowing light, thinking it would still appear on the back of her hand. It did not. It was not a reflection or even light projected through the window. When she lifted her hand off of it, the angel was still there. It was not a reflection off of a surface. The entire encounter shocked but amazed Andrea.

It was October. Arika was in bed listening to a Mariah Carey Christmas CD that she found when cleaning her bedroom. She called me in to tell me an angel was above her. Arika said his name was Judas, but he was not her guardian angel. This divine being loved Christmas music too. Arika carried on a conversation with the angel, but she never spoke out loud. AngelBaby's entire dialog was telepathic unless she spoke to me to explain the chatter. It was like I was telepathically impaired!

SUE QUINONES

Chapter 5

Seeing Spirits

How do you protect a child with a heavenly gift from negative energy? How do you also safeguard this child from undesirable influences in our society? We did not understand how to protect her, but we would try. Arika was two, so we filtered out negativity and evil-based media. I never let Arika watch movies about the horror genre, especially demonic films. I did not want to influence her gift as a small child in an undesirable manner. Or place ideas in her mind that did not need to be present.

I did not know what Arika saw or did not see unless I asked questions. When Arika was older, I had no problem letting her decide what she wanted to watch. It was the formative years that worried me. When Arika was of age, I hoped her gift would guide her.

Arika was two, Jose started to take her out in the backyard to play. She turned to Jose and said, "You don't have to come in the backyard because Papa is watching me now." I could not believe it! Arika never met my Dad or knew that we called him Papa. We never hung photos of my family members because Jose and I are artists, and artwork is up everywhere instead. Arika did not understand who he was or that he existed. My Dad was sick for over fourteen years, so I tried to forget all the sad memories.

Arika interacted with him as if she was his junior assistant. I would always see her talking to him. One day she declared, "I wish I could see how Papa looks?" I responded, "I thought you could always see him?" She whispered as if not to hurt his feelings, "Papa is a soft white shape. Sometimes I see him, and other times I feel him." Later that day, Arika told me she felt Papa was there in the room.

Arika said, "Papa is still alive. When you die, you just change forms."

Arika had just turned four years old when my brother John and Jose took her fishing. I thought she would never put a worm on a hook. She took the juicy worm and said, "Sorry, but it's time for you to get the fish." My brother and Jose laughed.

During the silence of fishing, you could hear a howling dog in the distance. Arika looked up at John and said, "That sounds like Papa's favorite cartoon." It shocked John! My Dad loved the animated series called *The Roadrunner Show*. You know the cartoon with the coyote who always gets hurt, and the roadrunner says, "Meep! Meep!" How would she know that? That show aired in 1966 and ran on television until 1972. AngelBaby never watched that cartoon. We never talked about what my Dad liked or did not like. He had died years before Arika was born.

When I was at school teaching, my Mom made Italian cookies that my Dad loved so much. Arika helped her twist the cookies. Mom's hands didn't work too well these days because her muscles were getting weak. Mom told Arika she was having trouble coiling the cookies. Arika instructed her, "When Papa was tired of making cookies, he made them into meatballs." She then made the rest in round balls of dough. Mom could not wait to tell me. We produced large batches of cookies for every holiday, and my Dad would make the remaining spherical. Mom forgot he did that until Arika reminded her.

It was Easter, and most of the food was ready. My brother, Bill, always cooked ham for all the holidays. He was sick, so I had bought the spiraled ham, but I never cooked one before. I didn't know where to start. I stood there staring at it, thinking about my approach to the situation. Arika walked into the room and disclosed, "Papa said to turn the ham upside down in the pan and sprinkle nails on it" (I figured she meant cloves.) I guess my dad was right there watching me cook for the holidays!

I took Arika to our favorite restaurant in Slavic Village called *Red Chimney*. Mom and I were sitting in the restaurant eating with Arika. Out of the silence, Arika said, "Papa says he loves you, Mary." Mom's eyes got big, and she smiled. I got goosebumps on my arms when this little five-year-old relayed the message to my mom. All of us in our family call her Ya-Ya or Mom. My Dad called her Mary. It was as if my Dad channeled through AngelBaby to give this specific message. My Mom was happy with Arika's communication from the other side. That small connection gave my Mom the strength to go on in life without him.

We went outside after Arika's first day of school to sit on the porch. There was a woman that lived three doors down from us. Her mother had died a few months ago. The older woman's dog died about six weeks before her death. AngelBaby was very excited as she stared at the park across the street. Arika stood up with excitement in her voice and said, "Look! She is walking with her dog with a smile on her face." I looked and looked and didn't see anyone. I said, "I don't see her." Arika replied, "Duh, Mom. It's her spirit!" First, my little kindergarten daughter just insulted me, and in my defense, I thought Arika was telling me about the woman's daughter, who also had the same last name.

One weekend in August 2003, there was a widespread power outage throughout the Northeastern and Midwestern United States. The disruption even reached parts of Ontario, Canada. It was getting dark outside. Andrea and I were lighting candles in all the rooms. Arika was playing with a flashlight and looked surprised when the light moved in a jerking motion. Arika uttered, "A spirit moved the flashlight. I guess it was trying to warn me that the lights were going to go out for a long time."

The lights flickered several times that Friday and were out for the entire weekend. As we were standing in the dark, Arika blurted out, "Do you guys want to meet my friends?" In unison, we yelled, "No!" Andrea and I feared that Arika was a magnet for spiritual entities, and these specters visited her more in the dark.

AngelBaby woke up Andrea during the night. Arika said there was a spirit in front of the window just standing there. Andrea turned on the light and surrounded Arika with angels, and they went back to sleep.

The next day, Arika sprinted downstairs. She said the spirit had returned upstairs. It made her emotions unsettled. Arika said she did not see it. She sensed it was there. We took the Holy Water and sent it to the light. We went through the entire house and blessed each room again.

After that, Arika was all right and never felt the undesirable force again. Arika saw spirits almost daily, but two souls startled her because they came out of nowhere. She was not afraid, just surprised.

At first glance, Arika seems like any other child until she expressed a message from God or has a quick glimpse of an angel encounter. Since none of you know Arika as a person, I thought I would tell you about one of the profound moments in her life.

Arika's wisdom was impressive. It was as if she has an old soul from a distant past.

Arika was around seven years old, and I found her sobbing in her room. I asked her what was wrong. She declared, "I love you so much, and I love my birth mother. I love you and dad for adopting me. You are the best mother, and I have the best family in the world. I also love my birth mother for giving me a chance to live instead of having an abortion. She gave me life. I love her for that." Then I asked Arika, "Why are you still crying so hard?" With tears, Arika interjected, "I am crying for all the children who died in abortions and did not have time to live." Speechless, with tears in my eyes, I just held her while she cried.

I want to tell you about an unusual spirit encounter while drying my tears from the last paragraph. Arika previously explained to me the difference between angels and spirits. Angels always hover, and their feet never touch the ground. They are messengers of God. They can never be relatives who have passed on. The relatives are spirits, not angels.

Unlike airborne angels, spirits can appear standing right in front of you. Apparitions of relatives can guide you in life. Souls trapped after death are ghosts. Arika said, "You must tell them to go to the light because they are stuck and don't know they are dead." AngelBaby told me spirits are relatives but can sometimes be unrelated spirits. It was the unknown spirits that left an impression on me.

Arika was playing upstairs in her bedroom, and I was doing laundry before bedtime. With excitement in her voice, Arika yelled, "Mom, I see dead people!" I thought I was in the movie entitled *Sixth Sense*. What is going on? Arika never saw that movie. Shivers went through my body when she said that. Taking a deep breath, I hesitated and then replied, "I'm coming!"

I entered the room and saw Arika staring at the mural my husband, Jose, painted for his AngelBaby. Filling the broad wall were two beautiful white horses, drinking water at the ocean's edge. A gorgeous sunset surrounded it. Arika announced, "Six spirits are looking at dad's painting right now." I tried not to freak out, so I interjected, "Maybe they are a bunch of dead artists." We laughed.

I asked Arika, "Do you want to sleep with me tonight?" She said, "I'm good." Well, I must tell you our bedroom is the adjoining wall, and I could not sleep all night thinking a gathering of spirits was in my baby's room. I was terrified of the anonymous forms, that's for sure. For Arika, it was just another day.

When you have a relative who dies and knows you have an extraordinary gift from God, spirits will search you out to give you a message. Or they just let you know they still exist. When Arika was a toddler, I remember her sitting on Jose's brother's lap. Rafael studied Arika, and he noticed how bright she was. He watched her rifle through a television guide, staring at all the pictures on each page. We told him about her gifts from God. Only our families knew about her unique gifts.

Years later, Rafael's died. Arika ran from the bathroom and articulated, "The weirdest thing happened when I brushed my teeth this morning. I was looking at myself, and my eyes changed into Uncle Rafael's eyes. Then I saw his face in place of mine." I inquired if he had any messages. She assessed, "No! I think he just wanted to tell me everything was okay." Jose's brother Rafael died in 2007 when Arika was nine years old.

My preteen Arika loved to go shopping with me to the local store down the street. We encountered this small cemetery countless times in our city during the day and night. One evening we passed the graveyard. Arika shivered and said, "There is an evil spirit." When she says something out of nowhere like that, you listen. It made me wonder why the apparition appeared to her right then. Was it waiting for an opportune moment to address her? Friendly spirits always greeted Arika, but this one had a foreboding presence.

Our family avoided cemeteries or any place with an excess of spirits. Spirit attachment was not an option for Arika. I remember a girl from my art class telling me that someone kept tapping her on the shoulder when she entered her basement. The weird thing was that she was okay with it. When Arika came to our school that year, she told the same girl someone committed suicide in her house, but he was harmless. However, Arika said to the student, "Never go into cemeteries because spirits easily attach to you. You might bring home an evil entity."

Andrea went on an excursion to the old haunted Mansfield Prison with her friend Beth from high school. She took pictures and caught some orbs in the rooms with her cell phone. When Andrea came back home, Arika told Andrea that a spirit followed her home. You got it! Holy Water throughout the house and on Andrea. We sent the soul to the light with prayer.

In 1909, the Cleveland company Glidden Paint built a beautiful home in the University Circle district. Glidden House served as the family's primary residence. The mansion was an impressive, influential home in the neighborhood. It contained dozens of rooms, a full basement, a courtyard, and a carriage house. In modern times, this home has been a delightful venue for weddings. It also acted as a majestic hotel to enhance Case Western Reserve University and University Circle's surrounding areas.

    My nephew and his wife had their wedding at Glidden House in 2015. Now a sixteen-year-old soon entering her senior year in high school, Arika was excited to go to the event. Our entire family attended the service and the following reception. Everything was great. We enjoyed the wedding, but Arika struggled in the environment. It overwhelmed her with the overabundance of dead relatives from the Glidden family. Arika was nauseous and disorientated. I took her to the main hallway. She and I sat in the chairs near the entrance for a while. We left a little early to escape the gathering of spirits that used her as a bridge to visit our dimension.

Chapter 6

Arika Goes To School

It was so challenging to send AngelBaby to school, where her family could not protect her. You would think that by my fourth child that I would have dropped her off at the door. Fear struck my soul at the thought of Arika encountering an opposing force. I felt helpless. I worried about her every day. Andrea, Jose, my Mom, Alena, and I were protective over Arika.

AngelBaby was like a sponge absorbing knowledge. She loved kindergarten and couldn't wait to get to school. I had to talk to her about her gifts.

Arika thought everyone had enhanced abilities. I feared the students would tease or bully her. AngelBaby's endowments were second nature, so she concealed them from others to live a normal life.

God put a protective bubble around her that young children could not sense. I observed the phenomenon when she went swimming. The children didn't know what was about to transpire. Arika moved close to the group of fellow swimmers. They shifted away as if not to infect her personal space. I was witness to it from the spectator's balcony several times during the sports season. After seeing the phenomenon, I let Arika take part in school activities. I knew that God would protect her from evil.

Arika came home from elementary school, exhausted. She told me she felt sick because something occurred. AngelBaby had a vision that an evil person was trying to enter the school. Arika had to put her head down on the desk because she was nauseous. She sensed the principal's anxiousness through an emotional connection. Did my baby also have the psychic ability to feel other's emotions and sensations through empathy? I believe we can just add that to her list of superpowers from God.

There was a man on the R.T.A. bus that shot someone and jumped off the bus. He was running toward the elementary school. The police were on their way. The principal handled the situation by putting the school in lockdown.

By fourth grade, Arika worried about the proficiency test near the end of the school year. Imagine perceiving all the things we see and have in this world, simultaneously observing the other side with spirits and angels around everyone from another realm. It is overwhelming and surreal. It upset Arika that she would not do very well in her testing. I told her to ask God for help in getting through testing. Arika prayed for her gifts to stop. She could test without distraction from the other side as her abilities disappeared. She received good scores on all the sections of her exams.

Two weeks after the school testing was complete, I found Arika crying. She had seen no angels. Arika feared she was losing her ability for good. I told her to pray to God so she would see them again. About three weeks later, Arika came running out of her bedroom. She had tears of joy because she saw her guardian angel hovering over her with enormous wings and luminous light. It was in silhouette, and Arika could not see the angel's face. She was so peaceful and happy. From then on, Arika could tuck the gift from God away and reveal it when necessary. It made her life much more manageable.

Arika was eating a snack after school. I inquired. "Do you see any angels at school?" Arika responded, "Yes! I see angels around students: not all teachers have many angels." She giggled.

During fifth grade, Arika had a teacher that she adored. She told me all the time how she felt the teacher was a wonderful person. The instructor's birthday was coming up soon. Arika asked me if she could give her a special present. She wrote a letter explaining her gift from God. Arika revealed to the teacher how many angels she had. She also included the angels that were surrounding her children. Arika gave her the letter after school. I came to the presentation for support in case I needed to help explain the message.

The teacher read the note. Her head tilted while emotions filled her expression with awe. Tears formed in her eyes as she finished reading the letter. Receiving the supernatural gift, she hugged Arika. Sobbing, the teacher cried, "It's the most fantastic gift I ever received."

I don't know if you were old enough to remember the incident, *Miracle on the Hudson River*. It was back in January 2009 with US Airways Flight 1549, coming from La Guardia with one hundred fifty-five passengers. The plane was only twenty minutes into its flight when it hit a flock of Canadian geese. It sucked the large birds into the dual engines, causing engine failure. Captain Chesley Sullenberger, designated as *Sully,* landed the airplane in the Hudson Bay, New York City, missing the George Washington Bridge by 900 feet (0.27km). I remember seeing the incident unfold on the news.

Jose and I could not believe it would take so long for the plane to sink while *Sully* and the crew helped everyone exit. The plane just sat there on the water. Our now eleven-year-old Arika was walking down the hallway. She peeked her head around the corner of the room and said in a disgusted tone, "I see two angels holding up the wings! That would give everyone enough time to get out. The plane would have been underwater already!" AngelBaby then finished on her way down the hall. Jose and I just looked at each other, and we thought it made sense.

Even while a preteen middle school student, Arika still enjoyed coming to my high school to do angel readings. A girl in my art class was pregnant. Arika told her the sex of the baby but interjected, "There are two babies." The girl replied, "Wow, you are right." Being so excited about the verbal confirmation, the pregnant mother of two invited Arika and me to her baby shower.

One art instructor at my school was pregnant. She asked Arika if she knew the baby's sex. AngelBaby sat back and closed her eyes and said, "I never saw a boy naked, but I think what I saw must be a private part. She is having a boy!" We all laughed.

Melissa had her baby boy as predicted and named him Joseph. When she was pregnant again, Melissa asked Arika if she could tell the sex of the second baby. Arika confirmed Melissa was having another boy. Afterward, Arika said to me that there was a problem with the baby. I told her it was best if she didn't worry Melissa, but maybe she could say something helpful for the birth. Arika told Melissa she needed to exercise. In a reassuring voice, Melissa said, "I'm on it!" She immediately started stretching.

Melissa's pregnancy seemed fine, but Arika told her the baby would be born early in March even though it was due in May. One day I went to Melissa's classroom to say hi. I realized she was not there. I thought Melissa had given birth to the baby.

After school, I took a walk with Arika in the Metroparks and told her Melissa was not at school. Arika stopped in her tracks and said, "It's all changed. Melissa is not having the baby early. It will be born in May because the baby's head is too big. She better pray to God like she never prayed before."

I went to school the next day, and Melissa told me she spent the day at the medical center, but everything ended up being okay. I did not want to explain what Arika predicted, but I felt it was an urgent communication. I articulated the message from Arika. Melissa listened to Arika's prediction. She responded, "Don't worry, I will call you as soon as I give birth."

Melissa went to the hospital in May to have her baby. The baby's head turned and could not pass through the birth canal. Doctors had to perform a cesarean section. The birth was rough, and Melissa prayed like she never prayed before. Her baby's lung collapsed, and he stopped breathing. It was rough for baby and mom. Melissa was in no shape to call me. James was finally out of danger, and Melissa was okay.

In the middle school years, Arika muddled through. She joined basketball, volleyball, and volunteer programs, mindful of her resume for college. She still visited my school every year to give angel readings for those who were interested.

Every time Arika came, there was always one or two readings that would stand out from the rest.

I remember a student who was released from jail still wearing an ankle bracelet. Arika told the student he had five angels protecting him. He asked if the angels would take a bullet for him. She replied, "No! They are there to guide you in making better choices, so you follow the right path in life."

One girl in my class was reluctant to request a reading. She finally did. Arika surprised her and declared, "Your mother is standing next to you. Your mom says she loves you very much!" The girl's eyes got big. The student said her mom had died when she was young. She always wondered if her mom loved her.

A beloved teacher and sports coach died at our school. The students were distraught over his death. Many of the football players said he was like a father. Arika has told me the coach's spirit was always roaming around at the school for all sports competitions.

They shot and killed one of my students in his neighborhood. When Arika visited my school, she noticed a handsome African American male spirit walking around in my class. He was waving with a smile as if nothing happened.

Arika's protective bubble from God disappeared after elementary school. She could now protect herself from the unknown. When Arika saw negative energy, she would tell it to go away. Life became manageable. We were still cautious, but we let Arika be on her own with her gifts.

AngelBaby was a well-adjusted teen in high school with good grades. Students elected her class president during her freshman and sophomore years. She helped to organize a parade and got the entire high school and local community involved.

Arika was a talented violinist and artist. She entered and got accepted into a National Art contest with her pastel drawing of an eagle. The artwork had the twin towers in the eye's reflection and an American flag shaped like a tear. The artwork reflected the terrorist attack on the United States on September 11, 2001, labeled as 9/11. Near three thousand Americans died in the incident, and many were left injured. Overall, Arika's high school experience was positive. She still found time to visit my school at least once a year to give her angelic readings.

AngelBaby visited New York City on a field trip where the orchestra got to play at a soup kitchen for the homeless population. For the rest of the journey, the musicians got to tour the city. Arika went to see the monumental tragedy of 9/11. Her empathy gift was in full use as she felt an overpowering sense of grief and an air of sadness lingering in the entire area.

During high school, Arika's premonitions happened more and more. She told me of a time when she had a Deja Vu moment. Before a basketball game, she dribbled the ball down the court, and she made eye contact with a boy sitting on the bleachers. She turned her head back and missed the basket. It was difficult for her to concentrate on the game. Arika forgot about the premonition until it all played out on the court. Ouch!

No one from high school knew of her gifts. Being intuitive, Arika would give friendly advice to others. Having these gifts from God gave her an edge on information from a different realm. Arika seemed wise beyond her years. I remember her stating, "People afraid of death are terrified of life."

Chapter 7

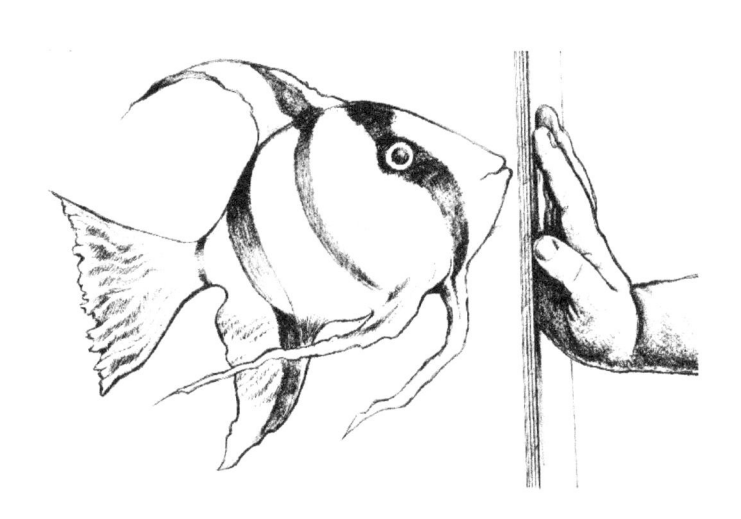

Fish Tales

It was a typical summer day of standing in line at the bank, shopping, and traveling from one destination to another. Arika was four. She came with me on my daily excursions. One of our errands was to meet Andrea at the research facility in *Rainbow and Babies Children's Hospital.* Andrea was finishing a medical project. We were waiting for her on the hospital's main floor.

There was a giant fish tank that seemed to occupy people sitting in the waiting area. While we were there, Arika requested, "Mommy, can I play with the big fish?" I answered, "Sure." The fish was on the other side of the tank. Arika ran to the opposite side and placed her tiny little hand on the cold glass. She smiled, and the angelfish scooted across the tank. It made a kissing motion against the surface, trying to touch Arika's hand.

AngelBaby smiled again and moved her hand to the side of the tank. The angelfish followed. I could not understand how she did that. I fixated my eyes on her and the fish the entire time. I tried to justify that it was a coincidence. Then it happened a second and third time. The angelfish followed her directions several times while Arika silently commanded the fish without verbalizing a word. The large fish moved to another location, trailing Arika's every move.

A five-year-old boy was watching AngelBaby. After absorbing Arika's encounter with the fish, the boy decided he wanted to have fun. He jumped up and shoved her hand off the glass, and shouted, "Let me try!" He put his hand on the transparent surface in the exact spot, and the angelfish swam away to the other side of the large aquarium. He tried over and over to get the fish's attention. The boy was mad.

What just happened? Did Arika have some kind of unique energy or telepathic gift to communicate with other creatures? Using telepathy was so alien-like, and no one could do that unless it were in a movie. Right?

I attempted to ask Arika to play with the angelfish again. Andrea popped out of the elevator, and Arika swiftly ran to her for a big hug. I didn't say a word to Andrea. I was in awe of the fish incident. How can a four-year-old child have the gift of seeing angels, seeing spirits, remote viewing, empathy, telepathy, and more?

Pondering what happened, I tried to analyze and come up with a reason for it all? I just couldn't. So, I documented everything on paper and let my thoughts go off into the universe, telling no one what occurred.

Years later, my daughter Andrea worked at a school with a dripping radiator in her classroom that formed a black mold on the carpet. At the end of the school year, she got pneumonia. It filled her lungs with fluid, and they admitted her to the hospital. The doctors had to do emergency surgery. While we were all in Andrea's room, Arika noticed my Dad, her grandfather. She called him Papa. Dad's spirit appeared in the hospital room. I didn't know if that was a good thing or not. I thought maybe he was helping her or possibly waiting to take her to the other side. Andrea had stopped breathing several times, and this was no laughing matter. She was in trouble. Who knew? I certainly did not know. Only God knew if she would live through the night.

While Andrea went to surgery, I took Arika downstairs to the first floor to a coffee vendor. I saw many people coming and going through the front doors. We sat down with a drink to wait. We talked about many things. Arika and I were never at a loss for words. We were best buddies. We discussed school, friends, and whatever popped into our heads at the moment. It helped to distract away from Andrea's terrifying situation.

I glanced across the room and noticed a fish tank with too many fish for such a small aquarium. At that moment, I had a flashback of the big blue angelfish's telepathic experience at *Rainbow Babies and Children's Hospital* from when Arika was four years old. Should I ask Arika to go to that fish tank? I hesitated to tell her because this memory of the angelfish was unknown to her. Well, why not? I have nothing to lose, right?

Arika was in the middle of rattling on a conversation and talking to me like she was seventeen instead of eleven years old. I interrupted her, inquiring, "Arika. Could you do me a favor right now? I would like you to go up to that fish tank and place your hand on the tank's side. Then, I would like you to talk to the fish with your thoughts." She answered, "Sure." I watched her, thinking nothing would happen.

Arika put her hand on the side of the rectangular aquarium. The fish were swimming then started flipping and twisting in the water. All the fish got in a linear formation facing her to the tank's right side as if they were frozen in time. They stood in total suspended animation! My eyes got big to view the whole craziness better.

I fixated my eyes on Arika. I wished at that moment that I would have taken out my cell phone camera to record the entire thing. The event lasted about fifteen seconds. Arika carried on with her telepathic conversation until her hand left the glass. The fish swam back around as if nothing occurred.

When she finished with her fish chat, she came and sat down next to me. I inquired, "What did you say to the fish?" Arika replied, "What's up, fish! How are you doing?" And AngelBaby rambled on and on about what she told them. It was time to write it down and figure out how Arika thought all this was normal. Insane as the whole scenario seemed, I was proud AngelBaby had so many gifts from God. She never thought it was unusual.

Fish were not the only creatures Arika contacted via telepathy. She loved horses. AngelBaby wanted to go for horseback riding lessons. How would I protect Alena from the horse allergy she had? I didn't want to put her life in danger. I had to figure out a solution.

I covered the interior of the car with fresh sheets. Arika would go to horseback lessons and sit on the sheets for the ride home. Now, Arika was near the door of the house. I stripped off all of her clothes and boots, surrounding her with the cloth sheet. I took everything upstairs to wash. AngelBaby jumped in the shower. It was so worth all the extra precautions to experience horseback riding each week during summer in Arika's eyes.

When Arika went horseback riding, she sat deep in thought on these glorious creatures. Her favorite was Rusty, but she also rode Millie and Spirit. They seemed in sync with her silent commands. I remember the instructor saying Arika has a way with horses as if they knew what they were thinking. I almost blurted out, Duh! She is telepathic! It was hard not to scream Arika's gifts to the world when I knew she was so blessed. Besides, I was proud. Arika not only loved horses but wanted her own until she took a job cleaning a barrel full of poop from the stalls! That cured her.

Occasionally, Arika would see cats roaming in our house. Let me clarify; the cats were spirits. Cats were the creature of choice that lingered from the spirit world. One night a cat crawled on Arika, and she thought it was hers. AngelBaby smiled when she realized it was the spirit of another feline. Well, at least in this house, spirit cats were abundant. Maybe the previous owner loved them!

When four years old, AngelBaby would play in the backyard by herself in the clubhouse that Jose made. She would sit on the lower-level deck and lay in the sun playing with dandelions and grass surrounding the perimeter. I watched her from afar and was shocked when a young deer approached her. Arika silently sat communicating with it. She gave a dandelion as an offering to the deer. I was afraid it would hurt her. I told AngelBaby it was still a wild animal, and she cannot walk around the yard with it as if it was a dog. Arika told me the girl deer was very gentle. Of course, Arika wanted to keep it.

Daily, AngelBaby sat and waited for her new friend. The deer came on several occasions to visit her. They seemed to have a silent pact together. Upset that it stopped coming, I explained it was time for the deer to go back to her family.

My mother had a dog named Tasha. She was a beautiful, fluffy huskie with a dark marking around the eyes in a mask's shape. Tasha looked like a raccoon. The dog was striking in appearance. When Arika was two, she would sit on the dog's back. AngelBaby would suck her thumb, feeling its soft fur. It amazed me at the dog's attachment to her. The dog just sat there and didn't care about the intrusion. It all made sense now when I think back at this dog following her all over the place. Was she telepathically talking to her? It was a possibility, for sure.

Tasha was only four years old. She was sick with an infection. The vet gave her medicine that shut down her kidneys, and it was too late before we realized what was going on. She died. Arika missed her furry friend.

I believe it was several years later when I was tucking Arika in bed in her cozy room. I felt a cold draft on my leg. It felt like ice. I looked down and then at the windows sealed tight. I tried to justify why a chill touched against my leg. Arika squealed, "Tasha, you came to see me." I questioned, "Where is she?" Arika said, "She is sitting right next to me on the bed." Arika touched the dog's fur, petting ever so gently. I squinted my eyes to see Tasha. I will never forget the chill I felt as Tasha brushed against me to jump on the bed to greet Arika.

Arika's best friend was our dog, Rosie, a Golden Labrador. They had a special bond. She had a thick rope attached to a bone that Rosie would grab. Arika would sit on a small blanket while Rose held the other end of the toy. Arika would tell her, "Go, Rosie!" The dog would pull her across the wooden-floored hallway while Arika would laugh. They played all day long.

Arika would wrap this giant Labrador from head to toe with toilet paper to fix her imaginary sprains and injuries. Rosie sat, waiting patiently for Arika to cure her. They sat in silence, without words most of the time. They were inseparable. How did the dog know her every move? One day I found both in the old training dog cage because I heard Arika barking. Of course, they were eating dog treats together!

To this day, Rosie's spirit roams throughout the house, freaking out the tiny Chihuahua we inherited from Jose's mom. The little dog was always biting Rosie's neck. This gentle giant just turned her head as if the small dog didn't exist. With fear on his face, the Chihuahua senses Rosie's spirit. There are rooms in our house this little dog is reluctant to go into during the day and night. Karma is rough, even on animals.

SUE QUINONES

Chapter 8

Rosa The Pig

A frequent question I ask myself. Does anyone believe in God anymore? I noticed that each year more and more students say they do not believe in God. Yet, they believe in aliens and supernatural things. Their parents do not instruct them about religion at all.

As a teacher, I witness so many students hardened by a tough life at such a young age. Some are homeless, verbally or physically abused, neglected, or victims of multiple marriages with wild stepfamilies. Many do not believe in anything at all, just themselves, and understandably so.

With the dawn of social media and cell phones, students withdraw from life's burdens and sink into their niche. Many use drugs to escape from reality. You will hear young people say they believe in ghosts, vampires, and paranormal entities, but seldom will they acknowledge God's existence. If they don't see it on their cell phones, they don't believe it. Is there a way to counter the total cycle of despair and lack of moral beliefs?

I treated my art class as a total learning experience, hoping to change some lives through intervention. I told the students that everything they do in life is for a reason, even entry into my art class. All the people you meet, good or bad, will be your lessons learned.

One of my wise students said, "Everything you go through in life is a lesson or a blessing." I know the basic quote was similar online to that concept, but he personalized it, so I considered it his original belief. So, besides our class conversations on the universe, I hoped Arika could help those floundering in life by setting them on the right track. Or at least get some of them thinking about something besides themselves.

Arika loved coming to school with me at least once a year when she was young. As the high school students in my art class entered, they observed my youngest daughter Arika sitting mysteriously behind my desk in a chair next to me. The previous day after school, I sprayed Holy Water around the room and prayed. I always protected Arika from the unknown.

Instructing them she would join us in class, Arika would not tell them anything unless they asked. I reiterated the rules and told them not to overwhelm her all at once. I had Post-it note pads ready and waiting for her angel count, spirits, and messages. You could see many apprehensive students, and even some were non-believers. We pressured no students into asking. It was their free will to make the connection.

I never heard the room so quiet. Everyone listened to Arika's answers as I wrote them on the post-it notepad. Silent students lined up just to listen and get a glimpse of this blessed child. Some took the note and stuck it to their shirt to show everyone the news when they left the room.

Gossip traveled fast, and each year the numbers increased with students from other classes sneaking out to see Arika in person. I felt her presence gave many students hope. Astonishment filled their faces. Many were perplexed with lots of questions to ask her. One-year students must have texted each other because my art room filled up to the brim with a line going out the door. I was sure I would get fired.

Arika made eye contact with them and then looked down as if she relayed a message in a trance. Arika told me, "I never remember what I tell them." It also seemed like she could not repeat the words for the students. That is why I started writing it down on small sticky notes.

One year when Arika came to visit, the Hispanic students were discussing the length of their names. They took turns telling each other in the group their first, middle, and last names. Arika leaned over, whispering in my ear, "Mom, I know my name! It's Arika Marie Gonzalez Quinones." I was trying not to look surprised at what she said. This nine-year-old knew her birthmother's last name.

I found the Gonzalez name the nurses forget to erase on Arika's immunization records by accident. When she was a baby, I constructed a letter for Arika to open on her eighteenth birthday to locate her birth mother. Wow, I admit, Arika shocked me with that one.

The following year there was a Hispanic student. He was so eager for her arrival. He made a list of questions to ask Arika. When he was a little boy in Puerto Rico, he would play with others in the ocean, picking up the small crabs along the water's edge. The boys would scream as the crabs would pinch them and not let go. The arthropods would lay quietly in the Hispanic boy's hands without harm.

The Spanish boy went back to the farm where he lived and pick up baby chicks that would not survive birth and cuddled them in both hands. It was like he breathed life back into them. He questioned his grandfather about this. The boy remembers his answer. You will meet a person someday that will explain to you what your ability is.

The student waited all day in my classroom while watching AngelBaby tell each person in line their number of angels that come and go to protect and guide them. Sometimes she would say their guardian angel's name, conveying that this special angel stayed with them from birth to death. Other students would have spirits of relatives as invisible mentors.

For instance, a relative like a grandparent or an aunt guided them in life. Sometimes you would hear Arika give a distinctive message from beyond. One student's memo was ominous. It didn't mean doom and gloom were evident. Arika would say it is up to you to use your free will to change your life outcomes.

Another student, whose name is not essential, but his timeline for solving his dilemma was imperative. Arika advised him, "As soon as you finish high school, you must get a real full-time job, or what you are doing now, you will do the rest of your life." Arika and I did not understand what it meant. He sighed with hesitation and whispered, "I sell drugs." I paused, then uttered, "I think the key phrase *rest of your life* probably means your life will not be too long if you stay on this path. I suggest you get a job immediately!" He was an outstanding student, and I think of him often. I wondered what choice did he finally select. Everyone has free will. It was up to him.

The day was near the end of the last-period class. The bell rang. Still waiting all day, the Hispanic student asked Arika his extended inventory of questions. Before she read the list, she declared, "God gives everyone a gift in life. It is up to you whether you use it. You have been given the gift of healing." The young man's face lit up with joy as she continued with all the answers to his scribbles.

I gave him a small sketchbook and told him to use it to date and journal his notes when trying to use his gift to help others. He came back to my class a week later to talk, and a girl was resting during lunch because she had a migraine. He asked her if she wanted help, and she agreed. The Hispanic student put his hands on her head and prayed. Within minutes, her migraine went away. He took out his book from his pocket and wrote some notes, and left.

Exhausted from the day's readings, Arika fell asleep on the car ride home. Doing angel work for people all day long took a toll on her. But, I was always thankful Arika came. I don't think AngelBaby knew her impact on everyone's lives.

The most memorable visit to our school happened on one fall day at the beginning of the school year. Arika was not in school yet, so I brought her with me. She sat in front of my desk. A student sat at the other desk next to her. He picked up some crayons and started drawing. The student wanted to talk with Arika. Before he could say anything, my AngelBaby looked up at him and divulged, "You have a pet that died." He replied, "Yes." I interjected, "Is it a dog or a cat?" Arika reacted, "No! It is his pet pig, Rosa!" The teen leaped out of his seat and paced around the room to tell his story. He captivated the classroom audience with his exuberant demeanor.

The student revealed, "When I was young, I lived in Puerto Rico for the summer with my Abuela. I loved it there and would play all day long. Then, one day she called me in to eat dinner. I was starving and told her the food was good." She retorted, "It should be excellent. It is your pet pig, Rosa!" So, she served my best friend for dinner!

The classroom roared with laughter. One student yelled, "Mrs. Quinones, why don't you get AngelBaby on *The Oprah Show* because she is fantastic!" I told him I didn't want to exploit her gift. Instead, just spread it around thoughtfully. Arika's final words to him were informative. She said, "Rosa loves you, and she is with you mostly in the morning and late in the afternoon. She follows you all over the place."

The next day the news spread like a California wildfire. All the grade levels heard the story. It was like AngelBaby was a legend, and it was unfolding in our school. It was Friday, and I brought chocolate chip cookies for anyone who wanted some. The student with the pig spirit walked in to visit. He smiled, picked up a few cookies, strolled out slowly, looked over his shoulder, and said, "Come on, Rosa, let's go."

Chapter 9

Angels Outside The Doors

I wish I had more answers to tell you about life after death. Death is one of the greatest fears causing anxiety. It provides you with an unsettling awareness of your existence in the universe. It encourages you to ponder life. Should I choose virtuous or troublesome outcomes? Your life is determined by how you embark on those journeys. The fact is, many people dip into the realm of negativity. Those choices add to the fear of the unknown and life as we know it.

My Uncle Ed just had a stroke. The doctors did not expect him to live for more than a week to ten days. My sister and her family took him in. We visited every day. Tears ran down his face, so we said the rosary to calm his fears. Arika came with us, declaring, "An angel is floating over him." Later that evening, Arika said she saw my Dad. My Uncle Ed and Dad were brothers, and I assumed that he appeared to help with my uncle's transition.

The next day we returned. Arika and I were driving to visit Uncle Ed. I asked her if she thought there would be an angel with him again. She did not know but said my Dad would be there. I questioned, "How do you know?" Arika countered, "Because he is in the back seat driving with us. Papa and I don't like that you are taking the long way to see Uncle Ed." I thought maybe AngelBaby said that because she knew he was going to die now. But, when we got to the house, Uncle Ed was still okay. I then realized my Dad always took shortcuts, making us go his way.

Now, Uncle Ed was too sick, and I did not want Arika to see him anymore. So, Andrea took Arika to visit Alena at college, where she was finishing up pharmacy school. They went to a carnival and slept overnight. I called the girls and then told Arika I missed her. She told me, Mom, if you miss me, pray to God, and then I will see you. Shocked at what she just said, I answered, "Okay."

Uncle Ed had taken his last breath and passed away. We would not take Arika to the afternoon viewing, but we brought her in the evening. I started to explain about death by telling her it looked like Uncle Ed was sleeping. Arika corrected me and said, "Mom, Uncle Ed's soul has left his body. Papa is arguing with him right now and wants Uncle Ed to go to the light. Uncle Ed is sticking around for a while. He is on his way to heaven with Papa, and that's why he is dead." This concept is hard to understand at any age. I guess she schooled me!

Arika went down to the basement level of the funeral home to get a drink of soda. Her cousin Kristin was sitting with her. Arika told her out of nowhere that Papa was arguing with Uncle Ed because he didn't want to go to heaven right now. Arika said Uncle Ed would have a sleepover today near his body and tomorrow promises to go to heaven. Kristin relayed the message to me.

Arika was in the viewing room with all of us. She told me that Papa was here to see his brother. I asked her where in the room he was located. Arika pointed to a large planter with orange flowers in it.

She said Papa was standing in front of it. I couldn't believe it. She could have picked any beautiful arrangement, but Arika picked the one I selected for my mother. I had ordered the offering and told no one. I thought she would say he was standing right next to the casket, but she didn't.

Jeanne's husband had a fatal heart attack from exerting himself with a snowblower during winter. Attending the wake, one of his daughters was distraught. Arika intervened, relaying a message from the father thanking his daughter for all she had done for him. Arika told her not to worry because he is not alone. His grandmother was by his side. This minor act of heavenly information that Arika revealed comforted the daughter.

Another time, a friend from college I knew had died. Arika was six years old, but she did not have any problem coming with me to the wake, so I brought her. It was pure curiosity on my part. This person lived a sinful life and did many things wrong. I wondered what happened to you when you die.

Life is weird. You try to justify it in your head to fit your needs, but I am sure what transpires is a different story. I always contemplated what materialized when you've done something horrible, like kill someone.

We sauntered into the room and saw some unsavory characters paying their last respects. I asked Arika if there were any angels near the person. AngelBaby exclaimed loudly, "That's weird!" I whispered, "What's weird." Arika looked perplexed and said, "The angels are outside the main glass doors. They won't come in." My stomach felt sick. I had a flashback of the movie *Ghost* with the demon creatures dragging the bad guy into the underworld. Unsettled by the thought, I quickly grabbed her hand. We left through the side door.

Chapter 10

Others With Gifts

As Arika said in the Chapter with *Rosa The Pig;* everyone has a gift from God; it's up to you to use it. How do you figure out your gift? Do you notice any curious things that seem to repeat or show up all the time? Just concentrate and think about all the unusual moments that have happened to you in your life. Are you clairvoyant, seeing visions or images like bits and pieces of a story? Do you feel other people's energy through empathy as if you are experiencing it yourself? Some people are intuitive; some have premonitions, dreams, nightmares with warnings.

Let us not forget astral traveling, auras, seeing shadows from the corner of your eyes, telekinesis where you can move or change objects at a distance through mental capacity, or sensing someone is near. Don't disregard *Deja Vu* when you sense something that has already happened or telepathic messaging without saying a word. Do you always feel someone near you that helps to guide you in life? I am sure I did not cover every single scenario. Just take ten minutes to think about it. What is your gift or gifts?

Arika's presence seemed to enhance our E.S.P. connections. My granddaughter Alexandria slept over the house many times. When she was around eight years old, Alexandria saw the spirit of a very tall man dressed in cargo pants. He had on a blue button-down shirt, appearing to wave to her from the hallway near her bedroom.

The apparition had a giant brown Afro similar to the artist Bob Ross. The next day, the soul followed her to school, materializing in a vacant seat to the right of Alexandria. He had a smile on his face.

Well, Alexandria's grandfather died in a car accident at the young age of thirty-seven. He had a gigantic Afro coming straight out of the seventies. Why was she able to see him? Alexandria never saw spirits before. I believe spirit energy zeros in on all of us in our location via Arika in my observations. Although I can't rule out, Alexandria might have some ability. She had seen angels in the past when she was young, as many children do.

Premonitions are commonplace to people in their dreams and nightmares. My daughter Alena had a nightmare about the tsunami in Indonesia before it happened. When Arika was three, she had a nightmare involving my youngest brother, John. An animated stuffed animal electrocuted John with a lightning bolt. Afraid of the dream coming true, AngelBaby told me about the entire ordeal. I checked the weather to see if there would be a storm that day. The forecast looked good all week.

I called my brother John and asked him what he was doing today. He said his clothes dryer had smelled weird, and he would be rewiring it tonight. I told John he better not attempt to repair it because Arika had a nightmare that lightning struck him.

John called an electrician to fix it. The main fuse box had a wire configured wrong. The electrician stated, "It's a good thing you didn't tackle this dryer yourself. It would have zapped you!" John couldn't believe it. Arika divulged to me many times she knows or sees things before it becomes apparent.

My mother and I had intertwined experiences in one from two vantage points. In my dream, the thought kept repeating itself over and over all night. My mom was facing me in bright light. She kept saying Sue, can you see Dad? Can you? I would always reply, no, I don't see him. Finally, my mom's arms stretched out, trying to reach him. I then saw the back of my Dad in a silhouette form. I yelled, "I see him!"

When I woke up to get ready for our trip to Florida, my Mom was not feeling well, and she passed out. We called an ambulance. My Mom had colon issues and had to go to surgery. It went well, but later on, her vitals started slipping. Mom stopped breathing, and the doctors were able to revive her. The hospital kept my Mom in intensive care for several days. It was their mistake to give her the wrong anesthesia when she had a form of *MS*. Mom remembers my dad's image standing over her. The vision faded after the doctors had been all around her. My dream matched her experience.

Dreams seem to be a familiar venue for many people of all ages. When I was in my twenties, I had a dream about an old house. It had thin weathered wooden slats painted gray. I saw my feet walking up the front stairs, but I was young in this dream. The shoes were small. I was six or seven years old. As I pushed open the front wooden door, I saw the furniture covered in white sheets. I remember pulling the sheet off of the rocking chair with my little hand. The chair was upside down with the date 1857 stamped on the bottom.

The staircase captured my attention. I saw myself shuffling up to the first bedroom on the right. Pushing open the door, I viewed the burnt room, exposing the blue sky. When I awoke, I told Jose about the entire dream, stating, "I will never forget that house as long as I live."

A few years later, we were driving near Ridge road on Memphis in Cleveland. I saw the gray house from my dream. A caution tape was across the entrance with a big sign declaring, *No Trespassing*

We turned into the long driveway, and Jose and my brother John ventured into the house. I refused to get out of the car. It only took a minute until the police arrived, thanks to a vigilant neighbor. The officer asked me what I was doing there. I replied, "You wouldn't believe me if I told you." The officers walked in and retrieved my husband and brother. All I could think about was trying to explain to my dad why my sixteen-year-old brother was in jail. The police only gave us a ticket where we appeared in court, with Jose and John receiving a two hundred dollar fine.

Jose told me it was worth the trespassing charge. The entire interior was empty of furniture. They walked up to the second floor. Jose realized the bedroom door on the right at the top of the stairs was in a fire, and he could see the blue sky through the crispy interior. How did I envision that? Could that possibly be a reincarnation from another time or a spirit signature?

My son Andrew also experienced a dream but didn't tell us about it. He came with us to Our Lady of Lourdes Shrine in Euclid on Sunday instead of going to church. Andrew drove separately and left after praying while lighting candles at the memorial. On the way home, this squirrel bounced across the freeway in front of our car. Jose changed lanes after looking in his mirror. He also turned his head to double-check, and out of habit, I did too.

Neither of us saw any cars. Then, as we moved over, a red car appeared. The man must have been speeding. We swerved back into our lane, and the red car spun out of control and did a 360-degree spin in the middle of the freeway. We thought he would be dead, and it was our fault. Then, I looked back in the mirror, and all the cars stopped. None of us got hurt. What a miracle!

When we got home, we said nothing to Andrew, but he seemed nervous. Finally, he said, "You guys have to be careful on the road because I had two dreams about all of you getting killed. Dad changed lanes, and the car rolled over." Andrew intercepted the two dreams, lit candles at the shrine, and prayed for us. The miracle was much appreciated.

By the age of ten, Arika received another Gift from God. It was the gift of envisioning auras around people. This unusual gift is thought to show emotional, mental, and spiritual levels forming an energy field around the body. I asked her where did she see the auras? AngelBaby explained, "I see the colorful impressions around my friends at school and even the teachers."

She also saw the light around Jose's head when he turned. I asked her what color it was, and she replied that it was white. Jose was blessed this week with good news about his painting in the Susquehanna Art Museum Exhibition in Reading, Pennsylvania. I think Jose was glowing with happiness! Arika told me that mine was white with aqua. I responded, "I hope my energy field had an excellent color combination!"

We did everything as a family and went for pizza every Friday evening. Traci, my brother John's wife, worked as a server. While in the restaurant eating, Arika asked if we ever saw spirits or angels. I told her I saw something but was not sure if it was a spirit.

One night I woke up and saw a girl near the door. She was wearing a white canvas dress with buttons. Her hair was medium blonde, straight, and to the chin. We had a cat, and I thought it was strange that the cat was sitting there looking, staring at the little girl—many times before, we could see this cat staring at nothing. I saw the cat sitting looking through the little girl. I woke Jose up to show her to him. She disappeared.

Thrilled because I saw something unearthly, Arika asked me to show her the spot where I saw the image. Arika questioned if I could see her feet. I said, "Yes." Arika noted, "Then it's not an angel because angels hover." She seemed excited to solve the otherworldly mystery. We went home. Arika closed her eyes and put her hands on the ground where I saw the little girl. Arika then told me the girl was here a long time ago before we owned our house. I believe this paranormal incident leaves a residual impression where people from the past cause energy signatures.

Andrea has the gift of healing. I remember one of my worst migraines while sitting in the parking lot at the doctor's office. I was too sick, and I could not remember how to drive. Petrified, I was staring at my cell forever, and by the grace of God, I figured out how to press the speed dial. Eventually, Jose answered his cell phone. I could barely talk. When my family came to rescue me, Andrea placed her hand on my head and prayed. Her hand felt warm, like a heating pad. Finally, the pain eased up enough to give me some relief until they took me home to sleep.

I had been going to a licensed doctor who gave up his career with a calling from God. I would consider this doctor a faith healer and medical intuitive who also practices Meridian Regulatory Acupuncture. I went to him for my migraines. Since seeing the doctor, my migraines had lessened. Arika was curious about his gift and wanted to come with me to my appointment. The doctor's wife was present and asked Arika how many angels she had. AngelBaby told her about the angels and her guardian angel also.

The doctor walked in at that moment. His wife asked Arika if she saw anything around the doctor. Arika looked up, and her body jolted back until she bumped into the door. She looked down, stunned by what she saw. Then, overpowered with a bright light, Arika saw a grouping of healing saints behind the doctor in a luminous glow that astonished her. I took Arika to the bathroom so she could compose herself.

Arika watched the doctor administer my care. The doctor inquired, "Arika, do you travel?" She replied, "Yes." The doctor countered, "Me too!" He explained about Astro traveling to help patients in need. They talked about many things. I felt like they were on a whole different level of thought, unknown to me.

Are they talking about Astral projection or travel? Astral projection is an intentional out-of-body experience that separates the physical body, assuming that a soul or consciousness can travel throughout the universe. Is this possible? Is Arika also gifted to have out-of-body experiences? Is she able to hang out with spirits at night and come back to her body? Is this proof when we die that our souls continue? Do we roam in other dimensions? The questions are endless. I wanted to discharge any notion of a child being able to do this, but then I remembered something that materialized when she was young.

Yes, Arika Astro projected or traveled at a young age. One day my Mom said someone kissed her on the cheek during the night. Andrea said someone pushed her hair back last night also. Arika was walking past the room and overheard them talking. She stopped, and Arika reacted, "I kissed you, Ya-Ya. I leave my body at night. I went to visit Andrea too." We all looked at each other. Could that be possible? Then Arika interjected, "You should try it." Everyone could do it. You visit other spirits, but you have to go back by morning, or you will be dead."

I asked this young six-year-old, how do you know about spirits traveling? AngelBaby responded by saying, "Spirits come out of our bodies at night when we are asleep. They party until morning, and they go back." I questioned, "How do you know that?" She retorted, "Papa told me!" Arika then walked away to play with Rosie while we all stared at each other in disbelief.

It was a Sunday, and we took Arika somewhere with animals for a fun afternoon. We were in the suburb of Rocky River and saw a pet store. We looked at all the pets. Arika wanted only to hold the dogs. She selected a small friendly dog that just made her eyes light up with love. I had told her we couldn't have the dog since we already had Rosie. She did not argue and returned the dog to the cage. We went for ice cream and ended our day.

It was time for bed. Arika came up to me and said, "Mommy, can I please have that puppy?" I replied, "AngelBaby, I am sorry. One dog is just enough." Arika rushed into her bedroom and found her shoes, placing them outside the door of her bedroom. Arika stated, "Don't move my slippers because I will visit my puppy tonight, and I need a place to land when I come back!" Shocked by what she just stated, I told her, "Fine. I will leave them right there."

Arika was not the only one who was intuitive. I believed that being intuitive had always helped me in life. There was one incident I did not see coming. I finished work and approached the highway when a loud stern voice said, "Don't get on the freeway!" Puzzled, I looked around the car, and nobody was there. The windows were closed. The radio was not on. Who said that? Was it a man or a woman? The weird thing was that I could not tell who or what it was. Well, that alarmed me enough to put my blinker on and proceed into the other lane. I then turned on Brookpark Road, not the highway.

I couldn't stop thinking about what had occurred. After driving for some time, I was approaching another entrance to the same freeway. I said out loud, "Is it all right to get on the freeway now?" Nobody answered, so I entered with caution. I looked to the left of the ramp. Sprawled across the road was a giant semi-truck lying on its side. I cried, realizing that I would have died in the crash if I had not listened to that divine voice.

In 1981 there was a theory that the brain's right hemisphere influenced the intuitive, creative capacity or artistic category of people, while the left hemisphere favored a more logical or analytical type person who pays attention to details. According to this theory, right-brain people have more focused E.S.P. gifts. Now current trains of thought say no, the brain function is equal.

In my opinion, I feel artistic people tap into E.S.P. more often or are more aware that they have a gift. Conversely, Extra Sensory Perception appears to happen less often for analytical individuals. For example, Jose and I are both artists, and our children have recognizable abilities. While adopted, this is evident with Arika, who still has substantial E.S.P.gifts and is versed in music and the visual arts. The same is true of many of our friends.

It was evening, and we took a car ride for ice cream. Andrew was with his friends and not traveling with us. When families go on an excursion, they play the license plate game, or I spy. Jose told us he had been practicing to turn off the street lights with his mind. I had witnessed him doing that many times.

Andrea and Alena accepted the challenge to turn the lights off using telekinesis. Jose, Andrea, and Alena took turns concentrating on street lights. Telekinesis is the power to alter objects at a distance using mental capabilities. Their primary goal was to get the lights to turn off. Yes, you got it. The weirdest unearthly game ever. I just watched as if they all were nuts!

Jose got the first light to shut off. Then Andrea and Alena tried. They did it! I didn't even try because I considered I was there to record the wild moment. The weirdest part was they all were so proud of their accomplishment of using telekinesis altogether. Finally, Arika declared, "I am going to turn them back on." Well, AngelBaby did light up the streetlights that her Dad and sisters had all worked so hard to shut off; therefore, I guess Arika won the otherworldly game!

Chapter 11

Miracle On Delta Flight 1230

Let us set the framework for Delta Flight 1230. The Atlanta Airport was closed for about four hours, stranding everyone at the main terminal. It must have been some significant storm cell to stop all travel for so long. It stretched from the Great Lakes down to the Gulf Coast. We were eager to get home after Jose's brother's unexpected death and had already been there two weeks too long. We boarded and sat in the plane for a long time and waited for takeoff from Fort Lauderdale, Florida.

The flight attendant ended up telling us we could get off the plane and eat until they received clearance to proceed. We were all okay with that. After we had gotten off the plane, Arika, Andrea, Jose, and I decided it might be our advantage to book a flight the next day and have family pick us up. We didn't want to stay all night at the airport in the stormy weather. We all agreed and got in line. Arika seemed super happy with the decision. While we were in line, I realized I forgot to put some of my migraine medication in my purse. I had to take medicine each night. Stopping it so fast could give me a seizure. I had left it in my luggage on the plane. It was our turn at the counter. Just then, the flight attendant announced we were boarding Delta Flight 1230.

Andrea texted Alena at work. She surrounded us with angels. Jose said we better get on the plane since I had forgotten my medicine. Nobody wanted to get on, but we did not want to alarm each other of our anxiety. Fear filled AngelBaby's face. She did not feel good about this flight. Arika whispered to Andrea that her knees were knocking together. Arika sensed we shouldn't get on the plane but didn't want me to go without my medication.

Andrea prayed the rosary to herself because she knew Arika's intuition was always correct. I thought that I didn't want it to be my fault if something happens on the flight. We all started up the ramp. Handing the ticket to the attendant, Jose had a flashback of a dream he had in his twenties. Jose remembered he dreamt he died in a Delta plane crash. Was today that day from his dream? Why couldn't Jose have recognized it three weeks ago when I booked the flight? I never booked a Delta before! Jose said to himself, "It's too late. I will have to leave it up to fate now."

Andrea sat by the window next to the wing. Arika was in the middle, and I was on the left side by the center aisle. Jose sat off to the right side of the plane on the other side of facing the center. I remember glancing over once in a while, looking at him. Jose drew portraits to pass the time to not think about the horrible dream. It was calm on the ground, but once in the air, it was turbulent. The storm was around us.

The lightning was illuminating the wing, and I was afraid it would hit the plane. The airplane dropped several times. Jose remembered the man sitting next to him, talking and saying, "Whoa!" The stranger reacted to the turbulence's motion as if he were on a roller coaster. Arika's calm demeanor turned frantic. She started sobbing and cried out loud, "I know God gave me special eyes, but I know what death is, and I am not ready to die yet."

Arika had said nervously she saw a vision of all the people dying, and it was just too much to bear. I leaned over to Jose and told him what she said. Jose covered his eyes with his hands and said, "Oh God, this is it. AngelBaby knows about my dream of perishing on a plane." I ignored Jose and tried to convince Arika that she could save us like she always did in the past. I told her, "God wouldn't give you special eyes if he didn't know you could handle it. You can do it, Arika." We held hands, and I grabbed Jose's hand. I didn't care who saw us hold hands across the aisle, praying out loud. Arika put her head down and prayed.

"Dear God, please surround all the people with angels to protect them in the day and night. God, please surround the airplane with angels to protect it. God, please surround my family with angels to protect them in the day and night. Amen.

Now things got strange. It was like we were in a soundproof chamber. It did not just get tranquil; dead silence filled the air. Arika shouted, "Did the engines stop, Mom?" I blurted out, "No! It can't stop!" All I could think of was us plummeting down into the ocean. There was a surreal stillness, and you could not hear the engines or the swoosh of air blasting from the overhead vents. No people on the plane were talking except Andrea, Arika, and me. There was no storm or lightning, no sounds or motion. Everything was still! What was going on? I never looked over to see Jose.

I focused my total attention on the three of us. Arika grabbed the brochure of the schematic for plane emergency evacuation. All I could think of was the picture of the floatation devices because my biggest fear was that I could not swim if we crashed into the ocean. AngelBaby stared calmly, pointing to the drawing of the plane. Arika then declared, "Two angels are holding up the wings. A giant angel with his arm outstretched above its head was holding up the plane from underneath."

Looking at Andrea, we sighed in relief, knowing we would be all right. Suddenly, there was a swooshing sound. Air vents were noisy again. The engine's resonance returned. The storm and turbulence vanished, and the rest of the flight was smooth. Arika was happy again. I was just glad we were all alive.

However, as we had that occurrence, Jose had his own experience. He had not heard Arika mention anything about angels. After I told him that Arika knew we would all perish, Jose put his head down and prayed the rosary.

Jose's right hand was on his metal pin attached to his collar, symbolizing the Holy Spirit. Keeping his eyes closed, Jose picked up his head, realizing time had stopped. He witnessed no sound from the air vents, no people on the aircraft, or engine noise. Instantly Jose found himself outside the plane, hovering in an out-of-body experience. Suddenly staring inches from his face was the wing. At the end of the wing was a beautiful angel with long hair.

Jose turned his head with his eyes still closed and turned left. There was another angel at the end of the left wing with long flowing hair and a white gown.

Then, Jose saw himself floating above the plane, looking down just in time to see a giant hand reaching up to the aircraft and grabbing onto it securely. He thought it must be the hand of God because he could not see the entire figure. Jose wanted to see more and then opened his eyes. At that point, Jose was returned to the plane but could not still see the man next to him. Jose looked down the aisle and did not see anybody in the seats. Instead of the storm, total silence filled the air. Jose thought to himself, "I must be dead. It's not bad being dead. It feels kind of good and feels serene." The entire event lasted several minutes. Then, unexpectedly, all the noise and people's voices came back. He said nothing to us. Jose said he forgot about the event until he stepped off the plane.

Jose told me something weird happened to him on the plane. I asked if he went through a void where there was no noise? We both started to remember something had ensued. He told me about his vision. I told him what happened to Arika and us. We had Arika draw what she saw. Jose drew what he saw. When Jose saw Arika's drawing, he laughed and said, "I guess it was a giant angel because all I saw was a giant hand. I just assumed it was God!" Jose never saw angels before and was so fascinated with the vision, as were we all. He took his and Arika's drawings and turned them into a large painting.

The effects of this experience lingered in our minds with a serene feeling of otherworldly calmness that lasted for several weeks. I interviewed each person to ensure I had an accurate account of that day and wrote the details exactly as they transpired to share this miracle. All I know that it was our destiny to be on Delta flight 1230 to assist everyone. We needed to pray together to ask God's messengers to help the people on the airplane. I know we were all blessed by God and surrounded by angels on that day.

Chapter 12

The Gifts Flourish

In these unsettling times, with everyone in quarantine from the *COVID-19* pandemic, I feel the need to say we have time to reflect on what is essential in our lives. We are witnesses to families with their loved ones. Most are wearing masks and maintaining a safe social distance. It has altered life. We spend our time in our houses with our families, staying vigilant. The virus has people reevaluating their quality of life. Many would love to establish a permanent home working environment. This opportunity is for those fortunate enough to have technology-based employment during the pandemic.

It strikes others in the population with fear. They lack essentials and healthcare. Looming eviction from their homes causes uncertainty in their future. The income disparity adds an unfair gap to minorities. Not everyone will fare so well from this unwelcome disease. All are in search of a miracle.

Miracles happen in our everyday lives, whether big ones like our Delta Flight 1230, divine intervention, or a random act of charity. We can all agree that the things that materialize on our paths in life are a surprise. It is how we face these challenges that make us the person we are. Asking questions about our existence and purpose in the world is innate. All people need to strive for answers and demand a rightful place in the cosmos.

AngelBaby's gifts flourish because of the need we have to question these unknowns. She is so blessed to tap into this realm. Arika bridges the gap between our world, aiding us to grasp a small precious glimpse of the other side. Hopefully, it will help heal our faith or prepare us to transition to our next destination.

Now in college, trying to figure out her career, Arika continues to live like all of us do, contending with life's choices. AngelBaby has the power to put her gifts away and take them out when needed. Arika seldom realizes the effect she has on people. Her abilities are built into her *DNA* from God. Arika still gets an occasional message from her angels or signs of a spirit around her, guiding her through life.

AngelBaby is private and humble about her gifts. The endowment to see even more visions ahead of time and telepathic connections are clear indications of Arika's ever-increasing capabilities.

Besides telepathy, AngelBaby has gained the gift of empathy. It is a form of *E.S.P.* creating a psychic link feeling other's emotions instead of thoughts. It can include physical sickness, anxiety, depression, or even pain. Arika sometimes struggles with this gift because the sensed experience feels like it is happening to her. Recently, Arika came to do readings at my high school. One student's life was in such turmoil that his intense emotions threw off her ability, and she had trouble reading others that day. The aftermath was draining.

Arika strives for meaning in life, never forgetting to be polite to people, and remembering nobody is perfect. Everyone you meet in life is for a reason, whether for a beneficial intention or dreadful result. Lessons can alter your life's perception. You can use your free will to find the correct path for you and embrace it with God's grace. Faith can help soften all that is wrong.

My life is a trek in losing faith, healing, and renewal. My significant life-long expedition is a journey of being the best wife, mother, and kind friend to everyone. I think that is what God is asking for us to do. God is not the person you blame when things go wrong. That is just life! God is always there to lend a hand in small but valuable amounts, even if you do not know that he is present.

Arika feels that everybody's placement on this earth is to fulfill a mission. Whether our purpose is clear cut, mistakes will occur, and lessons learned. They are not always significant life experiences. They can be minor acts ending in how you treat people around you with compassion. Creating complimentary messages and goodwill is one of the ways to send positivity into the universe. It will come back to bless you.

All the negative vibrations, however, return with substantial conflict and dilemmas. God is there to help you solve all the drama that life throws at you, but you must allow yourself to choose the correct path while spreading benevolence and love. As we try to realize our gifts from God, it is always essential to use them for good.

Blessed with many abilities, Arika is sure the messages are connected, whether decent or damaging, causing a chain reaction thrown into the cosmos.

I must state my final thoughts and hope I gave you some insight into a heavenly gifted child's journey. Everything that I witnessed and documented was very incredible and sometimes unbelievable, but so true. I wish you could have observed some of these little bits and pieces of the mysterious or touched a halo of an angel.

I believe this true story will help to give you AngelBaby's glimpse into the unknown. Hopefully, it will increase your curiosity to think about your life and how you fit into the big scheme of things.

My family feels blessed and gives thanks to God for allowing us to be a part of this little girl's life. Why our family? Was it all in the timing, or was it just part of God's immense plan?

I thank her birth mother and birth father for their unknown role as biological partners to create a beautiful baby girl sent to us with God's gifts.

Please think about your gifts from God and cherish them because you are blessed. God is always present in our lives, even if we can't see him. Some experts say that everything in nature vibrates at a different frequency. What if God has always been in front of us? Do we need to align our lives on his wavelength by living a good life? Will our positive vibrations raise us to his level so we can finally see God?

Did you ever throw a rock in a pond and watch the ripples gracefully echo out into large circles?

AngelBaby reminds us you are the rock, and the water is all you do in your life. All the culminations of your actions cause a critical chain of events. Your positive and negative choices will determine your contribution sent out into the universe. Use your life wisely.

ANGELBABY

Made in the USA
Coppell, TX
18 August 2021